-AN EPIC TALE OF INDIA-

FOR THE BRIDES OF GOPALPUR

-UMME RAZA-

ISBN: 0615942997

ISBN-13: 978-0615942995 (Umme Raza)

DEDICATION

To my mother,
who regaled our childhood with stories of Gopalpur
To my grandmothers
And to Haji Asadullah, our ancestor

৶৽৻

Dear Reader,

This petite "paper weight" in your hands as you may
    read and see,
Is Umme Raza's attempt at narrative poetry.
It was an enjoyable endeavor,
But hard, as one of the first tries ever.

To write a story was the plan devised at first,
But then came the idea of story-in-verse.
Penned at the author's age of eighteen
'Til now this poem was widely unseen.

A Note: You may find that many of the lines do not
    look at all even
However, with the same number of syllables each
    two lines were weaven.

৶৽৻

The fireflies swoosh up and down in the heat,
Lighting up areas oil lanterns don't reach.
The heavy night air cloaks the gathered girls & women
Who are settling themselves amidst all the joyous din.

They are about to listen to this village's defining story
That is recited to bless the Bride, to ward off similar
*   worry*
An elder around the time of each wedding portrays
How a Hindu, how a Muslim, had both others saved

(And an example of tolerance for Modern India made)

Gopalpur, the word that is the name of this rural
*   village,*
Has a history behind it, of honour, of blood spillage.
Located in the north-eastern province of Bihar,
Gopalpur's calm nights streak with star after shooting
*   star.*

Thus, it is difficult to comprehend that at this place,
Where women have surfaced with silk, satin, and
made-up face
Merrily wearing their finest twenty-two karat gold,
Many years ago, a story so sad did here unfold.

Behind the speaker are an old mud brick house and a
well.
Both are empty, as far as in this dark I can tell
The house has been maintained for three centuries
Decay is not allowed to visit with ease.

Let us take a few steps forward on the firm ground
And remove our shoes, and settle comfortably down
On the thin woven straw mat on top o'the fragrant
grass
As the elder tells what took place here 300 years past:

On the ground where stands the next town's school
Stood the huge home of a Tyrant cruel
Whose rule was on the local level;
Whose rule was like that of the Devil.

In his butter-yellow flared tunic and cerise sash,
He ruled after his father merely to gain more cash.
The Moghul Emperor had India's supreme rule.
Did he know it would be stolen as "Britain's Jewel"?

This local Tyrant allowed act of loot.
He never settled any act of dispute.
In the high trellised walls of his fort,
His low day bed was throne to his court.

In his royal bath one dull day
He decided on a gross way
To fulfill his lust like a hound
(Was white marble bath, in the ground)

He then walked in the garden to and fro,
Until the horrified sun went below.
While amusing himself with a chess game,
He thought how to women obtain and maim.

Mouth stained red with *paan*'s areca nut paste,
He pulled his dagger from his red sash-waist.
The ceremonial weapon with white jade handle
Ruby-studded, was too fine for this vulgar vandal.

Enlightening his courtiers about what he had planned,
The Tyrant explained how he would from this day
    demand
That ev'ry nouveau Bride should first be brought to his
    court.
On the nuptial night, *another*'s new wife, at *his* fort...

Realize dread! He planned to each woman rape
And then send back home in such a disgraced state.
He would have her brought like a fruit, peel and eat her
    up,
Then throw away the pit, and return to his wine cup.

Did he care what consequence his actions would have?
This Tyrant did not any conscience seem to have.
Opium, wine, idle sport, were his life
He did not care about children or wife.

With above-mentioned dagger waving up high
The Tyrant warned his men that they all would die
If even one of them failed to comply
With his order. He knew the threat was sly.

He knew they would listen as they always did.
There was no way for the danger to be rid.
Soon the citizens were living in more fear.
Marriages were postponed for another year.

For they had learned by now from experience that
The Tyrant wanted to satisfy his palate.
When one, two, then three new wives were taken
They returned to their grooms all forsaken.

What was left of their lives, after debasement?
Six moons later, it was with much amazement
That local people witnessed wedding arrangements:
"That (Hindu) family will suffer derangement!"

Now, Family in question wished to rebel
Against this practice, no matter what befell:
"We'll ward off the abductors with swords and spears.
Our warriors will protect her, have no fear."

Invitations were given, mostly through house visits
With precautions not to let any news slip of it
To the ears of the Tyrant's men. No word left a lip
Whilst Bride-to-be had henna put on each fingertip.

The rest of her hands were also red with design.
With the leaves' green paste was drawn a flowering
        vine.
A party was held for this henna-applying time.
(Henna is also called *mehndi*, a word hard to rhyme)

The in-laws came on palanquins from out of town
Bringing with them sweets, jewels, and red bridal gown.
The gifts of musk, carpets, desks, and horses were
     brought,
Horses with garlands of jasmine, chains of gold wrought.

But ev'ryone knew all the finery in the land
Would be of no use in front of the abductors' band.
But the family had hope, especially the Bride
Wanting to start her new life, not sit in fear and hide.

The day of the ceremony was muggy and hot.
Everyone prayed the Bride would not be caught.
The sun shone hard on the new husband and wife,
Perhaps hinting what to expect from their life.

The speaker now winds her grey plait into a bun
The heat seems like this night there is light from the
*   sun*
She takes a few sips from nearby steel glass of water
Then she starts another story, about a Daughter...

The old house and well that behind me rest
To the facts of this story can attest.
About a white-bearded man, I now will tell,
Who owned our village's land, this house and well.

This Haji Asadullah was an honorable man
He was loved by all, even those whom he ran
On the farmlands. His reputation pristine
Was known of by strangers he had never seen.

His offspring consisted of one Daughter solo
Who was married and living in far-off borough.
Haji Asadullah had become quite upset
Upon hearing of the plans of Tyrant despot.

Luckily his land could not be taken.
The Tyrant would be very mistaken
In trying to expand his land by force
As Moghul reign's penalty was most worse.

Haji (who was Muslim) wished he could assist
Neighboring town in making Tyrant desist
In kidnapping of Brides,
In the ripping of prides.

On the ev'ning of couple's worried wedding,
Haji's Daughter was setting up soft bedding.
She was visiting her old home with baby son
While her husband was elsewhere getting business done.

Laying the seven-month-old on the bedcovers,
She fanned away the mosquito that *still* hovers
All over India, to this day
Looping here and there, this and that way.

When she had arrived, Haji had come outside
To greet her with joy. Since her mother had died,
Beside servant Gopal, her father lived alone.
She: "The only grandparent my son will have known."

Sighing wistfully, the Daughter then did brighten
After door opened and Haji invited in
Her hometown friends, married and single "amies."
That night friendship cooled the heat like a swift breeze.

Later with Haji the Daughter had a sweet chat
While drinking hot chai and peeling pomegranate.
She prepared for sleep and gazed up at the dark sky
Which twinkled with shooting stars and bright fireflies.

ॐॐ

"Only a few stars mark the night,"
Says the Tyrant's man best at fight.
As Commander he searches mark
Forced to go on this midnight lark.

Word had come to the Tyrant's ear
That a wedding took place near here.
Outraged at the news' delay,
Tyrant wanted to catch his prey.

By now, who knows where the couple are?
The Tyrant's men have been sent this far
To search each caravan on the road
And find the one that carries Bride's load.

The Bride and Groom, along with in-laws
Had kept thirty guards, in case out-laws
Upset their route. About Tyrant's men,
They figured there would only be ten.

Little did they know there would be all
The men brought in to the new Groom maul
For daring to try and escape back with wife,
To another township, to start a new life.

After the wedding ceremonies that day,
The couple for safety had been sent away
To return back to Groom's town after sun-down.
Everything was packed to go, even red gown.

The night was almost over, they were getting near
The Groom's territory, which had a ruler dear.
But they were not there just yet
A few miles had to be met.

Trotting the horses at a more relaxed pace,
Unaware of what they were about to face,
They did not know that the Tyrant's Commander
Had already guessed where they would meander.

The Tyrant's men were lying in wait
For this job they would earn a good rate.
When the doomed caravan arrived in that lane,
The dawn sky was blackening, starting to rain.

The Tyrant's men jumped out with bloody shouts
Waving their spears, within minutes those louts
Had massacred all the caravan's members
Killed the Groom's parents, thirty guards dismembered.

In all there were one hundred and one
Of the Tyrant's men. Bride did first run
Into the bushes. She tore off her jewels
On lane there was gigantic blood pool.

One of the guards did lie
Right where she was, right by
The bush, so for defence she took his scimitar.
Then with an instinct for survival, ran so far.

She ran and ran until the sun made a band
Of pink light to greet the colours of the land
That was around her. The Tyrant's men were
Taking a long time in looking for her.

They were busy at first collecting wedding loot
And then removing the bodies, to clear the route.
The Commander thought the Bride couldn't go
Far, as she was "only a woman low."

In fact this Bride was a woman quite high.
Why exists such disrespect, why oh why?
The Bride in question had gotten quite far
Each raindrop to her felt like pelting bar.

Her husband of a single day was now dead.
Her whole town would live more than ever in dread.
What had she thought, that things could really change?
This Tyrant was absolutely deranged.

By the time the rain had stopped, the Bride had seen
Folded roses, lilacs, a heady jasmine.
She saw these beauties through drizzling tears.
Her sobs as she ran were of grief, not fear.

After she ran blindly for over two hours,
She reached end of the forest, of her power.
Like a flower, she folded down to the ground
Relief, as she realized what she had found.

She had reached the estate of a man so pious
So good and kind-hearted, without unfair bias.
She had been here as a girl of thirteen
And with her father the whole estate seen.

This large estate, which is now our village own,
Was the estate of none other than the well-known
Haji Asadullah. By now he had awaken
For the prayer of morn, and a cup of tea taken.

After Bride got up and walked closer and closer to
The house, she saw a fountain sprinkled with petals few.
The fountain was at the front of the home,
And this was where she used to love to roam.

Walking to the door, the Bride felt freshly-made pain:
"Widow" was now her marital status' name.
Dropping the scimitar onto the dirt, she knocked
With cries. Her sobs reached the skies. Door was soon
        unlocked.

The speaker now signals for some more water.
"It is getting late, and hotter and hotter.
I will now make haste and tell you
What happened to the ladies two."

Haji Asadullah took the Bride in despite
The grave danger from the Tyrant's men that he might
Encounter if they were to find out where was the Bride.
Tyrant didn't bother Haji, here was safe to hide.

Haji's Daughter hugged and calmed down the Bride.
The Bride was feeling so queasy inside
Realizing what gross torture she had escaped
She could have been captured and by the Tyrant raped.

☙❧

The Tyrant was grumbling on his day-bed.
He wanted the Bride brought alive, not dead
Then he could torture her for all the secrecy
Was obeying her ruler an indecency?

The Tyrant's Commander realized his mistake
In not going after Bride right away, with haste.
There was so much ground that had to be covered
With one hundred men chase would not be suffered.

They would find her in hours with expert tracking
The Tyrant's men in training were not lacking.
Unfortunately this claim proved to be true
As they followed the Bride's trail right through and
        through.

At around mid-morning they reached Haji's land
The Commander then led to the house his band.
He felt no remorse for what he was about to do
It was simply a matter of sword strokes, one or two.

For aiding a runaway wanted by the Tyrant,
Haji Asadullah was stabbed, and the men went
To see if he had an heir that could claim
The estate. If so, the heir they would maim.

The Commander concentrated on the Bride
Tying her up and carrying her outside
All the while telling her what tortures she would
Endure when she in front of the Tyrant stood.

Now remember that Haji's Daughter was there
She was his child, his legitimate heir
But the Commander upon noticing her did
Not consider a woman an "heir" to be rid.

The Bride was thrown onto a horse and then
Taken to palace with half of the men.
It is too painful to even try and devise
What poor Bride went through the two days before she
        died.

This is not the end of the story, there is yet more
You must realize that hiding behind a door
Was Haji's Daughter gripping her baby
Petrified, she thought she'd be taken maybe.

The Commander had seen her while he was busy
Now he decided to use his time that was free.
The Tyrant could have that muddied Bride if he wished.
Commander wanted this one in embroidered stitch.

He went around through the large and light
Rooms, his men gathering all wealth bright,
Jewelry, ornaments, sandalwood trunk...
Commander closer to back of house sunk.

Daughter knew that her son had to be hid
As potential heir, he would have a bid.
Quickly wrapping him up in cloths to be warm in,
She ran out to back and put him behind banyan.

One of the men saw her moving outside
Haji's Daughter knew no escape like Bride
Was possible with this many men around.
Walking to well she heard behind her a pound.

There came the Commander with the Devil's own face
His intention was clear, with sword he lifted lace
Lace of her tunic's hem, and she knew
That there was nothing that she could do.

Nothing at all, nowhere to escape
No one to try and prevent this rape.
The Daughter could not bear at all to submit
To such violation, and began to hit.

Alas to no avail
Did Haji's Daughter flail.
She decided that she would rather die
Than be treated this way under Earth's sky.

Crying to think of hidden babe's state
Daughter gave a kick to change her fate.
She hurried over the wall of the well,
Praying "God, please save my baby," she fell.

The Commander stood holding sword in shock
For only seconds, then back he did walk
To the house to look through the loot pack.
The group of men died on the way back.

Deceased Groom's town ruler had found out
What took place and sent own men on route
Of the Tyrant's men, to kill each murderer,
Which they did, returning loot of each burglar.

But that was only half the men.
The Groom's ruler then did pen
A letter to the Moghul Emperor,
Describing effects of Tyrant's temper.

After some weeks later Emperor did send
A troop of royal soldiers to descend
Upon the Tyrant's very palace
To end disgusting acts of malice.

The Tyrant and his men were killed
All three townships with joy were filled
Joy that was intertwined with much sorrow:
Innocents would not return on morrow.

One more person to be explained:
Haji's grandson, heir of land famed.
This babe behind banyan lay there until
Servant Gopal came back from flour mill.

He had left before came any sun's ray
The mill was over two hours away
Now coming back he saw the blood spillage
Saw his master dead, men doing pillage.

From behind row of banyans around the house,
Gopal worried about babe, helpless as a mouse.
Daughter was gone somewhere, that was apparent
But what about babe, was he gone with parent?

Just as Gopal was about to leave,
Grief with tears causing Gopal to heave,
Instinct told him to walk the whole
Line of banyans, with silent sole.

This he did, and was glad because
Lying on moss at back there was
The baby son so small, tired from
Weeping, cold, he was almost numb.

Gopal took him and escaped through
The Forest, as a hard wind blew.
Servant Gopal at this time was twenty-three
And engaged to a woman named Anjalee.

Gopal took the baby to his own parents' home
Which was humble but which eventually was known
As the baby's own abode. You see, Gopal did adopt
The baby, and so did Anjalee, the wife he soon brought.

Gopal took care to the baby raise
In solid Islamic Muslim ways.
Even though Hindu himself was he
Gopal respected Haji's fam'ly

When the son was already fifteen years,
On anniversary of Day of Tears,
Gopal took the boy to the edge of the wood
Where the Bride with heavy scimitar had stood.

This was the place where one could and can still see
All the land that was estate owned by Haji.
This day it was raining, but Gopal still did tell
Outdoors the story of mother's descent into well.

One of the Commander's men 'bout to be killed did tell
How Daughter drowned herself, was not pushed, into the
     well.
All the information was gained by the Groom's ruler's
Men, when they were busy slaying the murderers.

Thus Gopal now knew all, and all he did tell
To son of the woman who jumped in the well.
Son's father had never come to the town
Having heard and had a nervous breakdown.

Ev'ryone had thought that even baby was dead
Gopal did not dispute this to save baby's head
For he knew that there still existed those
Who wanted on the Haji's land a hold.

After telling the story, Gopal did look
Up at the now-dry sky, and a deep breath took
As the son pieced his history together
Gopal realized the change in the weather.

The rain had stopped, and the sun had now come
The sun was shining and for a welcome
It spread its rays upon the land.
Gopal showed estate with his hand

To give a gift to the young owner, the sun
Whispered with the sky. In seconds it was done:
Here was an arch of glorious colors
Spread over former land of boy's mother

Land that she owned for maybe half an hour
That she passed on to her son, and the power
That he had over it he used on his tour
Of his estate to name it all "Gopalpur."

As you can see the house is still here, well now without
     water.
Gopalpur is still here, un-owned by family of Daughter.
This is our village, and how it was named
Let us remember to keep rulers tamed.

Let us pray that this beautiful bride
Will never have happiness deprived.
For world's women, in our own respective way
Whether Hindu or Muslim, let us all pray.

ॐॐ

The elderly speaker soon gets up from her place.
She picks up a woven straw fan and fans her face.
The audience rises, murmurs, bids farewell to the bride
They return to their homes, taking the lanterns inside.

৶৽৶

(But we decide to do something different.
Heard tale first time, we can't be indifferent.
We go over to the well and take a peek
Feeling too spooked by what we just heard to speak.

Shine flashlight down into well,
What do you see? Please do tell...)

Join the book's fans online!

facebook.com/Forthebridesofgopalpurbook

twitter.com/forthebrides

Print and e-book copies available at

www.amazon.com/For-Brides-Gopalpur-Umme-Raza-ebook/dp/B00H2B6JW8

www.ingramcontent.com/pod-product-compliance
Lightning Source LLC
Chambersburg PA
CBHW060617030426
42337CB00018B/3093